Samuel Morton Savage, William Ford

Good men dismissed in peace

Samuel Morton Savage, William Ford

Good men dismissed in peace

ISBN/EAN: 9783337223663

Printed in Europe, USA, Canada, Australia, Japan

Cover: Foto ©Lupo / pixelio.de

More available books at **www.hansebooks.com**

Good Men difmifs'd in Peace.

A

S E R M O N

Occafioned by the

D E A T H

Of the late REVEREND

DAVID JENNINGS, D.D.

PREACHED TO

The CHURCH of which he was PASTOR,

SEPTEMBER 26, 1762.

By SAMUEL MORTON SAVAGE.

To which is added, A

FUNERAL ORATION

AT HIS

INTERMENT.

By W I L L I A M F O R D Junior.

Both publifhed at the Requeft of the faid CHURCH.

LONDON:

Printed for J. BUCKLAND, in Pater-nofter Row ; T. FIELD,
the Corner of Pater-nofter Row, Cheapfide ; and
S. GARDINER, in Grace-church Street.
M.DCC.LXII.

A

S E R M O N.

THE intimate connection in which, for many
years, I had the honour to ſtand with the
late Rev. Dr. *Jennings*, has devolved upon me
the ſervice of paying him this laſt public tribute
of reſpect; a *ſervice* which that connection, and
my regard to the requeſt of his worthy family,
would not allow me to refuſe with decency, tho'
I engage in it with much concern and diffidence,
and intreat your *candid* attention, while I endeavour to lead your thoughts to ſome ſuitable me-
ditations, on thoſe words which you have in

LUKE ii. 29, 30.

Lord, now letteſt thou thy ſervant depart in peace,
according to thy word: For mine eyes have ſeen thy
ſalvation.

WE learn from the context, ſee ver. 21, &c.
that according to a law of *Moſes* re-
ſpecting firſt-born children, our bleſſed
Saviour at about ſix weeks old was carried to the
temple at *Jeruſalem*, to be preſented to the Lord.
And behold, there was a man in *Jeruſalem* whoſe
name was *Simeon*; he was a juſt and devout man,
waiting for the conſolation of *Iſrael*; and the

Holy

Holy Ghoſt was upon him. And it was revealed
unto him by the Holy Ghoſt, that he ſhould not
ſee death before he had ſeen the Lord's *Chriſt*, or
that divine Saviour whom the ancient prophets of
the *Jews* had foretold and promiſed, and whom
he and other pious *Jews* were expecting to be
manifeſted, as the author of joy and conſolation to
Iſrael. And he came by a particular impulſe of
the Spirit to the temple, at the time when the pa-
rents of *Jeſus* brought him there. And immediately knowing who the child was, he took him
up in his arms, and bleſſed God, and ſaid, ' Lord,
' now letteſt thou thy ſervant depart in peace ac-
' cording to thy word : For mine eyes have ſeen
' thy ſalvation.' This good man appears to have
been advanced in years, drawing towards the uſual
period of nature, and ripe and ready for his diſſolution. But having had a divine promiſe, that he
ſhould firſt ſee the expected Saviour come in the
fleſh, he ſeems to have been ſome time waiting and
longing for this happy event; and now it was arrived, he expreſſes his readineſs immediately to
quit this world, in which he could look for nothing
elſe worthy his notice, after his eyes had been
bleſſed with this divine ſpectacle, after he had ſeen
and embraced *Jeſus*, the Saviour of his people.
" Now, ſays he, O Lord, thou haſt fulfilled thy
" promiſe ; for I have ſeen him whom thou haſt
" ſent to be the author of ſalvation ; now thou art
" pleaſed to diſmiſs me in peace ; this was all I
" waited for, and now my diſmiſſion from the
" world is welcome." Thus the primary meaning

ing of the words is obvious ; but they will admit being confidered with greater latitude, as applible to other good men in later ages ; and may furnifh us with this general obfervation, *viz.* " That " the fervants of God, who have feen his falva- " tion, are ufually difmiffed by him in peace.". Hence I fhall,

I. Briefly ftate the character of a *fervant* of *God.*

II. Shew what *God's difmiffing* his fervants in *peace* may imply.

III. What is meant by *feeing his falvation.* And,

IV. What *ground* that affords for a *peaceful difmiffion.*

I. Let us briefly confider the character of a *fervant* of *God*, and to whom it is applicable. A fervant of God is fometimes ufed in Scripture as a title of *peculiar honour*, fignifying one employed by the great God on fome *fpecial, important occafion* * ; as our great officers of ftate, and prime minifters are often called the King's *fervants.* So our *Lord Jefus Chrift* himfelf is emphatically called God's fervant (*Ifa.* xlii. I.) fo was *Mofes*, his type ; and fo the Apoftles call themfelves fervants of God, or of *Jefus Chrift* † ; as they were the principal minifters in erecting the gofpel-kingdom. And in this view, the fame appellation is fometimes

* See Mifcell. Sacr. v. 2. p. 12—15.
† *Rom.* i. 1. *Tit.* i. 1. *James* i. 1. *2 Pet.* i. 1.

given

given to the Prophets under the Old Teftament, and to the Minifters of the gofpel under the New, as in 2 *Tim.* ii. 24.   So *Simeon* might ufe it of himfelf, on account of his bearing a kind of *prophetical character* ‡; or perhaps he might only on *this particular occafion* come under a fpecial, divine illumination, and then the term may be taken here in a larger fenfe, as meaning *good men* in general.   This is indeed its common acceptation in Scripture.   By *fervants* of God we are therefore to undefftand *good* perfons, or fuch as, like this *Simeon,* are *juft* and *devout,* (ver. 25.) fuch as have a holy fear and reverence of the great and bleffed God, for the ruling principle in their hearts and lives. This principle was frequently ufed for the whole of religion under the Old Teftament difpenfation, as good people were then more commonly ftiled the *fervants* of God ; while under the New Teftament they are ufually honoured with the title of God's *children,* in whom *love* to him is fuppofed to be the ruling principle.   But though that love, which is the chief fpring of evangelic obedience, cafts out flavifh fear, there is a holy ingenuous fear of God, confiftent with true love to him, which is an effential part of the religious character under the gofpel, as well as it was under the law, and which refults from confidering ourfelves as his fervants and children both.   So the Pfalmift calls upon the Saints both to fear and love the Lord, and with fearing him joins hoping in his mercy, and fpeaks of himfelf as God's fervant, devoted

‡ See *Saurin's* Sermons, Vol. V. p. 58.

to his fear. To be the fervants of God then is the character of all good people, or belongs to all fuch as have an ingenuous reverence for God wrought in their hearts, governing their other affections, and producing a humble chearful fubmiffion to his will, and a regular courfe of obedience to his commands; to fuch as do not wilfully break his laws, nor habitually neglect any of the duties of religion, but heartily endeavour to do the whole of their duty, and glorify God in the world, and are fincere and faithful, though they are always ready to acknowledge themfelves imperfect and unprofitable fervants. But I fhall not enlarge further on this common topic, that I may have more time for confidering thofe particulars which are more peculiar to the text; efpecially as one of them, *viz.* feeing God's falvation, will alfo afford us a general defcriptive character of good people, more peculiar to the Chriftian difpenfation. We are then,

II. To confider what *God's difmiffing* his fervants *in peace* may imply. And here let us,

1ft. Enquire into the import of *God's difmiffing* us. Lord, now *letteft thou* thy fervant *depart*, more exactly, thou *difmiffeft* thy fervant. It is a difmiffion from the prefent life, from this world and all its concerns, which is here intended. And this is reprefented as the *act of God**; it is *He*

---

* *Saurin*, Vol. V. p. 59.

A 4   who

who difmiffes us from life, who gives us *leave* and *power* to die.   Now this intimates two things ;

1ft.   That life is to be confidered as a *ftation and fervice*, which we muft not *quit*, till we are difcharged from it by the authority of God, who has affigned it us, till *he* gives us *leave* * to depart. So good men are ftiled in the text the *fervants* of God, and he is ftiled their Lord, or *Mafter*, as the original word † particularly means.   This world is but a large family, which belongs to the great God, which he fuperintends, and in which all men are but his fervants, who have particular parts allotted them by him to fill up, and particular duties to difcharge, relative to the good of the whole.   None of us live to ourfelves, or die to ourfelves ; but living or dying we are the Lord's. He has an abfolute right to difpofe of us ; to employ us in his fervice as long as he pleafes, and to difmifs us from it when he pleafes.   He has given us all, as well as our bleffed Saviour, work to do here : and we muft not grow weary of the difficulties of our place, nor impatient to quit it, till we have finifhed our work, have ferved our generation according to the will of God, and glorified him thereby ; then like our Saviour, *we* may alfo befeech our heavenly Fat.er, to glorify us with himfelf, *John* xvii. 4, 5.   So *Job* fpeaks of accomplifhing as a hireling his day, Ch. xiv. 6.

---

* See *Stockius*'s Clavis of the New Teftament, in the words απολυω, and αναλυω, or p. 648.

† See *Paffor*'s Lexicon on the word δεσποτης.

Till

Till the fervice of the day is over, we muft not
look for the evening of reft; but as foon as our
work is done, God figns our difmiffion, that we
may reft from our labours, and go to receive our
reward. ‡ Some of the antient philofophers ufed
to reprefent men as in a *military* capacity, who
have various pofts affigned them, which it is their
duty to maintain, till they have the leave of God
their commander to quit them. ˙And the Scripture ufes the fame allufion, when it tells us˙of a
warfare appointed to man upon earth, *Job* vii. 1.
And fometimes it reprefents life, in allufion to the
Grecian games, as a *race* fet before us, a *courfe*
God has appointed us to complete : till therefore
we have finifhed our courfe, we can make no pre-
tenfions to the crown. And whatever difficulties,
danger, or oppofition we have to encounter, we
muft not inglorioufly defert our *poft*, or neglect
the duties of it, except we would meet the awful
refentment of him, whofe fovereign will has
placed us therein. Further,

2dly. God's *difmiffing* us may intimate, that the
prefent life is a ftate of *confinement, reftraint and*
fuffering to good men, from which God gives them
enlargement by death. The Greek word in the
text originally fignifies, the *diffolving* any fort of
connection, and therefore it is naturally ufed for
fetting at *liberty*, or *releafing* from *bonds*, as in *Luke*

‡ See Dr. *Clark*'s Evidences of Natural and Revealed Religion, Prop. I. Or, Dr. *Watts*'s Works, Vol. II. p. 363, 4.
Alfo the Somnium *Scipionis* in *Tully*.

xiii. 12. *Heb.* xiii. 23. and elſe where. And óne
of the Greek hiſtorians * applies it with this ſigni-
fication to *death*, which he calls a diſſolution of the
bonds of the body, or a diſmiſſion from them.
At preſent, the connection of the ſoul and body is
ſo cloſe, that the latter has a great and almoſt ir-
refiſtible influence on the former, and ſo debaſes,
depreſſes and enfeebles its nobleſt powers and fa-
culties, that the multitude of mankind lead no
other than an animal, or ſenſual life, and the people of God find great difficulty to maintain and exercife their ſpiritual life, and to prevent their being
quite overcome by bodily paſſions and appetites.
They feel continual reſtraints and checks upon
their divine affections and aſpirations, and perpetual impediments to their growth in grace, and
the improvement of their minds in knowledge,
piety and virtue ; and therefore they cannot look
upon their preſent embodied ſtate, but as one of
confinement and ſuffering, from which they would
be glad to be enlarged. And it is *death* that gives
them releaſe, by diſſolving the union of ſoul and
body, and putting a ſtop to all the influence of
this ſenſible world upon their immortal ſpirits.
And ſometimes their ſenſe of the trials and troubles of life, and the impediments, ſtruggles and
oppoſition they meet with in religion, are ſuch,
that they even groan under the burden, and wiſh
and long for the kind deliverance of *death*, to
give them an immediate entrance into the world

* *Arrian,* ſee *Stockius* ubi ſupra,

of

of perfect holiness and happiness, and to the blifs-
ful prefence of their Redeemer, 2 *Cor.* v. 1—8.
But it is their duty and care not to be *impatient*,
but to wait *his will* and *pleafure*, to wait *his time*
for their releafe out of this world, who fent them
into it. So fome of the heathen philofophers,
particularly Plato and his followers, reprefented
the body in the prefent ftate, as the prifon of the
foul, into which it was fent to do penance for the
fins of a pre-exiftent ftate;* and juftly argu-
ed, from this falfe principle, that we are not
to break prifon and run away. Though when
divine Providence does itfelf offer us a juft occafion of leaving this world, as when a man choofes
to fuffer death rather than commit wickednefs, a
wife man will then indeed joyfully depart, fays one
of them, as out of a place of forrow and darknefs
into light; yet he will not be in fuch hafte, as to
break his prifon contrary to law; but will go
when God calls him, as a prifoner when difmiffed
by the magiftrate, or lawful power. And again,
fays he, unlefs that God, whofe temple and palace
this whole world is, difcharges you himfelf out of
the prifon of the body, you can never be received
to his favour. And furely *Chriftians* fhould learn,
with humble fubmiffion and patience, to wait *his
time* for their enlargement, *whofe will* fixed the
bonds of the body upon their fouls, and who
alone has the right to loofe them; who has the keys
of *Hades* or the invifible world, and of death, the

* See *Clark,* or *Watts* ubi fupra.

entrance into it; who fhuts and no man can open, and opens and no man can fhut. Our times are in *his* hands, who has all fecond caufes and inftruments under his controul: we are all immortal, till he figns the warrant for our difmiffion, and *then* no man can redeem his life, or prolong his continuance here. With refpect to *death*, though fo defirable an enlargement to good men, we fhould learn to fay, with an excellent perfon of the laft age *, Lord, *when* thou wilt, and *how* thou wilt. When *death* therefore is fpoken of, as *God's difmiffing* us, it intimates, that the prefent life is a *ftation* and *fervice*, which we muft not quit without his *leave*; and a ftate of *reftraint* and *fuffering*, from which it is his *prerogative* to releafe us. We are to enquire,

2dly. What is meant by God's difmiffing us *in peace*, as he does his fervants who have feen his falvation. Now this implies,

1ft. With refpect to their *ftate*, that God removes good people out of this world, not in a way of *anger*, but of *mercy* and *favour*. The original word which we render by letting us depart, as it fignifies diffolving any fort of connection, is apply'd to *legal obligations*, and fignifies *remiting debts* and *punifhments*; as in *Matth.* xviii. 27. *Luke* vi. 37. and fuch a meaning it will bear in the prefent cafe. Tho' all men are debtors and criminals in the fight of God, and fin and the

* Mr. *Baxter.*

curfe

curse of his broken law firft introduc'd death into
the world, and the wicked are arrefted by death,
to be thrown into the prifon of hell, are driven
away in wrath, and hurried to the place of torment and punifhment; yet there is *One*, who has
born the curfe, and fuffer'd the bitternefs of death,
for all that believe in him, and has made them
the friends of God; *Jefus Chrift*, that *Juft One*,
who fuffer'd for us the unjuft, to bring us to
God, to procure pardon and acceptance with him,
for all penitent finners. To *them* therefore death
is fent, not as the executioner of the vengeance
of an incenfed fovereign, but as the meffenger of
a kind, merciful father, who, having forgiven
them all their offences, and being fully reconciled
to them, will not let them continue any longer in
this ftate of banifhment from his prefence, in this
ftate of diftance from their delightful home; but
fends death to remove them from a world, which
is too polluted and wretched to afford them reft,
where they can't be happy, and could not bear
to continue always, to bring them home to himfelf, in a world of perfect holinefs and happinefs,
a world where their treafure and their hearts are,
and where they defire to be for ever. He fees
they have finifh'd the work he gave them to do;
and he fees fit they fhould have no farther trials,
but commiffions death to admit them to their
everlafting reft and reward. Death is among the
all things which are *their's* thro' *Chrift*, 'tis a bleffing of the new covenant. Death in fact is *always*
an act of mercy in God to good men, as it deli-
vers

vers them from the fins and miferies of this world, to take them to the happinefs of another world. And *very often* the death of good people is fo *tim'd* and *circumftanc'd*, as to difcover much of the peculiar goodnefs of God, in taking them away from the evil to come, from fuch public, or family troubles, or from fuch perfonal trials of painful diforders, debility, and incapacity. for ufe-fulnefs, as they might have great room to expect, and as would have been extremely diftreffing to themfelves and their friends. God's difmiffing his fervants *in peace* then fignifies, his removing them hence by death in a way of *mercy* and *favour*, to take them to himfelf. This is the firft and *chief* thing to be regarded in death. But,

2dly. It is to be further obferv'd, that being difmifs'd in *peace* may refpect the *temper*, with which good men are difpos'd to meet death. It intimates, for inftance,

1ft. That they *acquiefce without reluctance* in the good pleafure of God, to remove them out of this world. This is a happy effect of religion, which is generally to be obferv'd in pious perfons. " The end of the upright is " peace," *Pfal.* xxxvii. 37. Whether they have the joys of *lively* hope or not, truly good people, if they enjoy their fenfes, have ufually calm, peaceful frames in their latter end, and are enabled to refign themfelves up to the difpofal of God, as children in the hands of a wife and tender parent. The

The *wicked* have no *reason* to be willing to die, to quit all their comforts, and go to meet the anger of an offended God, and be doom'd to endless misery. And with what reluctance and agonies are they often seen to make their exit! But divine grace, that has form'd the *Christian* to resignation and obedience to the will of God during life, will seldom suffer him to be so much under the prevalence of melancholy doubts and fears, when death approaches, as not to exercise the same graces then. He can trust that God with the care of his soul in the other world, who is Lord of both worlds, and has been his guide and support in this. He can follow him thro' the valley of the shadow of death, who has carried him safe thro' the dangers and difficulties of life. He believes that infinite wisdom and goodness cannot have order'd his death wrong, and is therefore ready to receive the notice of it, with a " Lord, " thy will be done." Tho' *Christians* are not to be *weary* of the duties and trials of life ; sure they will accept release from them chearfully, and will be ready to give up their difficult service, whenever God sees fit to employ them in it no longer, to quit their dangerous station, when 'tis not necessary for them to maintain it, and to part with the bodies of their vileness, infirmity, pain and temptation, and with all their connections to a hostile, ensnaring world, as soon as ever the great Disposer of all events thinks proper to dissolve them! This world can never be a very desirable place to serious *Christians* ; and therefore when
they

they have gone thro' their part in it, they will welcome their difmiffion from it, and be glad to hear their heavenly Father call them hence. So St. *Paul* was not only *willing*, but very *defirous* to die, 2 *Cor.* v. 1—8. *Phil.* i. 23. Which leads me to obferve,

2dly. That good men fometimes enjoy very *lively hopes*, and *comfortable, delightful profpects of heaven*, in a dying hour. They have good reafon to be refign'd to death, nay to wifh and long for it, as they are fometimes enabled to do, becaufe it is the means of their greateft good. Death is not the friend of *nature*, but of *grace*, for it violates *nature*, and deftroys the union of its conftituent parts, and was brought upon it as the penal effect of fin; therefore nature can but view and dread it as it's worft enemy; and wicked men, if they have any thought about them, commonly meet it with terror. 'Tis *grace* only can enable us to meet it with pleafure, and, thro' a triumphant Redeemer, to triumph over all its frightful forms, and view it, as in reality, a kind friend and benefactor, as the final period of all our forrows, and the never to be forgotten æra of our higheft joys. When *Chriftians* have the ferene poffeffion of their minds, and are clofing a life that has been exemplary for piety and virtue, and has afforded them long experience in religion, and the habit of faith has grown ftrong and vigorous, for the moft part they have the comfort of it's lively exercife at laft, and it exerts itfelf to the utmoft,
when

when 'tis juft going to be loft in the world of
vifion. The Scripture lays it down as a general truth, " That the righteous has hope in his
" death," *Prov.* xiv. 32. and 'tis commonly veri-
fied. The *Chriftian* receives his difmiffion, as
from the hands of his reconciled God and Father.
For his faith in *Chrift*, and the redemption thro'
his blood fpeaks peace to his confcience, and dif-
arms death of its fting, which is the curfe of
God's broken law. He dies in the favour of
God, and with a comfortable fenfe of his love;
and he believes, that the love of the eternal God
cannot be exhaufted by what it has done for him
here, but will do infinitely more for him hereafter.
He has a firm faith, in the promife of eternal life
to all *Chrift's* difciples, and a good hope through
grace that he himfelf is one of them; and therefore he can rejoice in hope of the heavenly glory.
And fometimes the comforting, fealing influences
of the holy Spirit are granted to departing faints,
in fuch a large meafure, that they have not only
the *witnefs* of their relation to their heavenly Father, but alfo the *earneft* in themfelves of their
heavenly inheritance, and can fay in full affurance
of faith, that they *know* they are going to a better
world, a world of perfect peace and joy; and
their faith almoft making up the want of fight,
they can rejoice in the *foretafte* of the bleffings of
which they are going to take poffeffion, and triumph in that beloved Saviour, whom they are
juft ready to behold! How peaceful and joyful is
many a *Chriftian's* death! And that is very com-

B   fortable

fortable and animating to furviving friends. But
when this is not the cafe, it fhould not occafion
doubts and fears about the fafety of their ftate;
as the graces of *true Chriftians*, particularly faith,
the moft neceffary in this cafe, are not always in
lively exercife, and their frame of mind depends
much on that of their bodies, whofe diforders
may impair their reafon, or quite take away their
fenfes.   I proceed now to the

IIId general head propos'd, which is, to fhew
you what may be meant by *feeing God's falvation.*
" Mine eyes have feen thy falvation," fays good
old *Simeon*, while he had the bleffed *Jefus* in his
arms; and therefore falvation, by a common figure
of fpeech, feems directly to mean the Saviour,
or author of falvation.   But *Simeon* ftyled him
fo, from a prophetical knowlege of the falvation
which he was to be the author of to all people,
that fpiritual falvation, in which *Jews* and *Gen-*
tiles and all his people partake, fee ver. 31, 32.
As we can't at prefent fee the Saviour himfelf,
but *may* fee his falvation, and *muft* fee it, if we
would be difmifs'd in peace; let us briefly confider,

1ft. *What this falvation means*, or *wherein* it confifts.   'Tis no mere temporal deliverance, as the
bulk of the *Jews* expected from the *Meffiah*; but
a fpiritual falvation, as *Simeon* under divine influence defcribes it, to be a light to enlighten
the *Gentiles*, as well as the glory of *Ifrael*, and as
Zacha-

Zachariah had before defcrib'd it, to confift in
remiffion of fins, and giving light to them that
fit in darknefs, and in the fhadow of death, and
guiding their feet into the way of peace, *Luke* i.
77, 79. 'Tis in fhort, the falvation that is in, or
by *Chrift Jefus*, with eternal glory. Now this falvation confifts more immediately in deliverance
from *fin* ; as *Chrift* was to be call'd *Jefus*, the Saviour, for this very reafon, that he was to fave
his people from their fins, *Matth.* i. 21. 'Tis
but initial in this world, and is to be completed
in the other. At prefent, *Chrift's* people are freed
from the *guilt* of fin, there's now no condemnation to them that are in him ; God forgives them
all their iniquities, and is reconcil'd to them, and
grants them much peace of confcience, and confolation in *Chrift*. They are alfo at prefent freed
from the *dominion* of fin. Sin does not reign in
their mortal bodies, has not the dominion in
their natures ; becaufe they are not under the law,
which only commands, without giving help to re-
fift fin, but are under the grace of the gofpel,
which gives life and ftrength to fubdue our corruptions and overcome temptations. This falvation further confifts, in deliverance from all
the *penal effects* of fin. The troubles of life are
falutary corrections, not curfes to true *Chriftians* ;
and death is but their gate to blifs. They have
God's favour and bleffing, his holy image and
likenefs, for part of their prefent falvation. And
hereafter, their falvation fhall be completed, in
their utter deliverance from the apprehenfions of

B 2   guilt,

guilt, the indwelling, the occasions, and all the effects of sin, and in their perfect conformity to God, and their full, uninterrupted, everlasting enjoyment of him, in a bright and blissful world. Such is the import of salvation; which we may observe,

2dly. Is *God's* salvation. The text is address'd to *God*, when it says, " mine eyes have " seen *thy* salvation. As *Jesus Christ*, the Saviour, is himself *God's*, is his son and his gift; so the salvation we have thro' him is also *God's* salvation. The great God is the original author, and his glory is the ultimate end of our salvation; and he is to be supremely acknowleg'd in the whole of it. So the apostle teaches us to trace up all its blessings to him, as their author, sum and substance, 1 *Cor.* iii. 21, 23. All things are yours, whether *Paul*, *Apollos*, or *Cephas*, that is, ministers and religious ordinances, or the world, or life, or death, or things present, or things to come, all are yours, and ye are *Christ's*, and *Christ* is *God's*. Nothing less than the infinite wisdom and mercy of the Deity, could design and contrive the wonderful scheme of our salvation; and nothing less than his almighty power could carry it into execution, and carry it on to it's perfection. He who was with God, and was God, the *Immanuel*, immediately and in his own person reveal'd salvation and procur'd it for us; and he begins it in us, and will advance and perfect it, and bestow all it's glories upon us. And God himself will be the

life

life and fubftance of our complete falvation, of
our bleffednefs in heaven; whofe rivers of pleafure flow from his right hand, and whofe fulnefs
of joy is conftituted by his prefence. *He* is the
portion of his people, and their exceeding great
reward. For when falvation is ftyl'd *God's* falvation, it may intimate it's *greatnefs* and *value.* 'Tis
fo great falvation, that an infpir'd writer could not
find an adequate epithet for it; 'tis one of that
infinite excellency, value and extent, that is worthy of the infinite God to contrive, accomplifh
and beftow upon thofe for whom he has the greateft
affection. But let us attend,

3dly. To what may be imply'd in *feeing* this falvation. " Mine *eyes* have *feen* thy falvation," is an
emphatical pleonafm, frequent in the Hebrew,
tho' not peculiar to that language. *Simeon literally*
faw and embrac'd the Saviour, which 'tis impof-
fible for us to do; but *he* could only by *faith* difcover the future falvation, of which *Jefus* was to
be the author. Therefore as apply'd to falvation,
and expreffing fomething common to all good
people, *feeing* it muft be underftood *figuratively*;
and it's import may be compriz'd in the two following particulars,

1ft. *Believing* in God's falvation. Looking to
Jefus the Saviour is us'd for faith in him, as me-
tephors borrow'd from the other fenfes have alfo the
fame application; and beholding his glory, as difplay'd in the glafs of his word, is put for believ-

ing it, 2 *Cor.* iii. 18. So to fee that falvation which is in and thro' him, fignifies having a firm belief and perfuafion of it. Faith is the leading grace in the chriftian life, and the firft requifite to our partaking of faving bleffings. They that dif-believe and neglect the great falvation, cannot be partakers of it. But fuch as would enjoy an in-tereft in it, muft ferioufly confider their need of it, attend to its evidences, meditate on its fuitable-nefs, fulnefs, extent and freedom, and be con-vinc'd of its divine appointment, that it is pro-vided for fuch as they are, and that *they*, weak and indigent, finful and unworthy as they are, may freely partake of it. As feeing is one of our principal means of obtaining the moft fatisfactory knowlege of things, fo the ufe of this expreffion here, may intimate that *confirm'd* belief, and *full* perfuafion of the truth and excellency of the gof-pel falvation, which folid and experienc'd *Chriftians* have, and which is neceffary to a *comfortable* death ; for though fafety after death is very confiftent with doubts, peace and comfort in it require faith without wavering.

2dly. To *fee* this falvation alfo implies an *expe-rimental* acquaintance with it, or an *experience* of it, and *participation* in it. It is not a mere fpecu-lative belief, that comprehends all the true *Chrif-tian*'s prefent concern with the gofpel falvation, and prepares him for peace and comfort in death. *Simeon* not only *faw* but *embraced* Chrift; and the ancient Patriarchs, whofe faith is celebrated in the

11th

11th of *Heb.* are faid, not only to have feen the
promifes of falvation afar off, and to have been
perfuaded of them, but alfo to have *embraced*
them. What St. *John* fays of himfelf and the
other Apoftles, 1 *John* i. 1. is applicable in a fpiritual fenfe to all true believers, they have not only
heard, and feen with their eyes, and looked upon
it, but their hands have *handled* the word of life :
or according to another fcripture metaphor, they
have *tafted* that the Lord is gracious, 1 *Pet.* ii. 3.
they have had a participation and experience of
Chrift's faving benefits. They have believed with
the *heart* unto righteoufnefs. Their minds have
been firft enlightened with the knowlege of the
truth as it is in *Jefus*, and their judgments convinced
of their need of him and his falvation. But this
is not all, here they have not refted; for then they
would fall fhort of falvation at laft. But their
will has been brought over to approve and accept
of *Chrift* to be their Saviour, in the way of the
Gofpel, to be their Saviour from fin itfelf, as well
as from its punifhment; they have been enabled
to receive him, and give up themfelves to him as
fuch; their defires and affections have been ear-
neftly drawn out after him, and the bleffings of
his falvation, and they have had fome pleafing experience of and delight in them ; at leaft this has
been the cafe with them fometimes, and efpecially
in advanced and eftablifhed *Chriftians*, who are
ready for a peaceful difmiffion. Such have received *Chrift Jefus* the Lord with a cordial faith, which
has commenced a vital union betwixt him and

them,

them, and according to the gracious tenor of the gofpel-covenant, has given them an intereft in all his faving benefits, or has actually begun his falvation in their fouls. They have received the forgivenefs of their fins, and they have received the Holy Ghoft, who has renew'd and fanctified their natures, and transformed them in fome good meafure already into his holy image. All the graces of the fpiritual life have been formed in their hearts and tempers, and are daily improving and carrying on to perfection by their divine Author, as the evidence and pledge of their future poffeffion of eternal life, or of that complete and glorious falvation in which they now believe, of which they are heirs, and for which they look and long. To *fee* the ·gofpel-falvation then as true *Chriftians* do, is both ferioufly to believe the fcripture revelation of it, and to have an experience of its commencement, by a work of renewing grace in our own fouls. I am now,

IV. and Laftly, To fhew you what *ground* this will afford for a peaceful difmiffion ; ' now letteft thou thy fervant depart in peace ; *for* mine eyes have feen thy falvation.' Whenever the *Chriftian* can adopt this latter part of *Simeon*'s fong, he can alfo adopt the former part of it: whenever he can fay, that he has feen the falvation of grace, he can alfo fay, that he is ready to depart in peace, and can rejoice in the hope of glory. The one is the ground of the other. Their *connection*, or the dependance of our being difmiffed in peace, upon
our

our having feen God's falvation, I fhall briefly argue and illuftrate in a few particulars.

1ft. Our having feen the gofpel falvation, as juft explain'd, or having believed in and partly experienced it, is a *reafon* of *God's difmiffing us in peace*; it is a reafon on his part, for granting us our difmiffion in a way of mercy and favour, and not cutting us off in wrath and vengeance. It is what carries in it the reafon of a *means*, and not of *merit*; for finful creatures, as the beft of men are, muft eternally difclaim all merit of theirs, with regard to God. But though we cannot merit any bleffings, in a way of *debt* from the juftice of God, we muft neverthelefs have a *meetnefs* for the reception of his favours, or his holinefs and wifdom will not allow him to beftow them; for we are to remember, that it is in all *wifdom* and *prudence* his grace abounds towards us, *Eph.* i. 8. He confers lower, to fit us for higher bleffings, the initial bleffings of grace here, that it may become him to crown us with the confummating bleffings of glory hereafter. Till therefore we have partaken of his grace, and his fpiritual falvation has been begun in us, we cannot obtain a peaceful difmiffion from him, and a paffport in death to the manfions of glory, prepared for his people. When unbelieving, impenitent finners die, they are fent to their own proper place, a place of torment, horror, and defpair; and till we have believed in *Chrift*, and accepted his falvation, we are all of us children of wrath, and cannot be in a ftate of

peace

peace with God, and therefore cannot be difmiffed by him in peace. But when we have believed in, and received *Jefus Chrift*, as our Lord
and Saviour, he is our *peace*, and by him we receive * *reconciliation* with God. It is *then*, according to the tenor of the new covenant, we are par-
doned and juftified by the blood of *Chrift*, are re-
ftored to God's favour, and renewed in his likenefs,
are adopted into his family, and have him, for the
God of peace, engaged to take care of us in life
and death, in time and eternity. Then death becomes a covenant blefling, and is fent as the meffenger of love, to put a period to our forrows
and troubles, our toils and conflicts, to give us a
releafe from our painful confinement, and an abundant entrance into the reft and recompence and
joy of our Lord.

2dly. Having feen God's falvation, believed in
and felt its power, *fits* us for dying in peace, with
refpect to our own *frame and temper*. It has a
fure tendency to do fo; and though a conftitu-
tional melancholy, the nature of the mortal difeafe,
or fomething fovereign and unaccountable in the
divine difpenfations, may now and then prevent it,
for the moft part it does produce this happy effect.
And that for very obvious and fubftantial reafons,
which I fhall briefly touch. As,

---

* So καταλλαγη fhould be rendered in *Rom.* v. 11. and not
by atonement.

1ft.

1ft. Becaufe having feen God's falvation is an
evidence of our being in a ftate of *peace with him.*
Though men can *live* carelefs and unconcerned
about the favour, or difpleafure of the God that
made them, what reafonable creature, in the ufe
of his fenfes, can *die in peace,* can think without
horror, of going to appear before God, as his judge,
and of being fixed by him in an eternal, unchangeable ftate of happinefs or mifery, while he is quite
uncertain, whether God is his friend, or his enemy?
But to have feen his falvation, to have been enabled heartily to embrace the Saviour of his ap-
pointing, and to have been renewed in the image
of his holinefs, is a clear, inconteftable proof of
his fpecial favour ; that his grace has made us to
differ; that with loving kindnefs he has drawn us;
that though we were enemies, we are reconciled
to him by the death of his Son, and that much
more being reconciled, we fhall be faved by his
life. For his love is unchangeable like his nature;
he will perfect that which concerns us ; and what
he has begun in grace he will confummate in glory.
And what abundant reafon is this, for the faint's
refigning himfelf to the cold arms of death without reluctance, with calmnefs and ferenity ? Nay,
what a firm ground does this afford for comfort,
joy, and triumph, in the profpect of his immediate
releafe from this enemy's country, to go home to
the everlafting enjoyment of his reconciled God
and Father!

2dly.

2dly. To have feen God's falvation, to have had his kingdom of grace commenced in our fouls, will *form* us to a proper *temper* for dying in peace. Where this fpiritual falvation has once come to reign in the heart, and wrought a thorough change in our nature, it will render devout refignation to the will of God, in all events, our prevailing temper through life. It will cure our immoderate affection for this world, loofen our attachments to it, and make us habitually ready to quit it, whenever infinite wifdom and goodnefs fee fit. It will make us meet for a better world, will give us lively profpects by faith of it's joys and glories, and will fill us with longing defires, with ardent afpirations after it, as our complete deliverance from all our corruptions, troubles, and temptations, and as the confummation of all our hopes, and wifhes, of our holinefs and happinefs. And then how welcome death! How chearful, how thankful the *Chriftian*, to fee his trials and conflicts juft over, and the end of his hopes and wifhes near! Further,

3dly. To have feen God's falvation, believed in, and experienced its gracious effects, will fit us for departing in peace ; as it will afford us occafion for the moft *comfortable reflections*, and give us ground for the moft *encouraging conclufions and expectations*. *Chriftians* who have feen God's falvation, efpecially if, like *Simeon*, they have arrived to advanced years, and have been long waiting for its completion, can look back upon many folemn

tranf-

tranſactions that have paſſed betwixt God and
their ſouls; they can recollect how often they have
ſincerely given up themſelves to him, through
his dear Son, both in public and private; what
delightful communion they have enjoyed with him
in his ordinances, and what animating inward
pledges they have received of his everlaſting love,
along with it's outward emblems, at the table of
the Lord. How often, when they have ſealed to
him a covenant of faith and obedience, has he
ſealed to them a covenant of promiſe and grace!
And they have therefore his unchangeable promiſes, his covenant engagements, to plead and
rely upon, for his never leaving nor forſaking
them, for his ſupporting and comforting them,
when they are to walk through the valley of the
ſhadow of death, for his being the ſtrength of
their hearts, when fleſh and heart are ready to fail,
and being their portion for ever and ever. Once
more,

4thly. Having ſeen God's ſalvation, is a neceſ-
lary *preparative* for the *ſealings of his Spirit,* which
will render death not only peaceful, but triumphant. Where our ſupport reſts only upon rational
deductions from, and applications of, ſcripture
promiſes to ourſelves, as anſwering the characters
of the perſons to whom ſuch promiſes are made,
it will be but weak and wavering; becauſe our
knowlege of ourſelves is ſo imperfect and unſa-
tisfactory, as our characters are ſo mixed, and our
frames ſo variable and inconſtant. A *lively joy* and
ſtrong

ftrong confolation, in the folemn period of nature's
diffolution, muft arife from the influences of the
bleffed *Spirit*, witneffing with our fpirits, that we
belong to the family of God, and are heirs of his
glory, and fealing us as fuch to the day of public
redemption. But in order for the holy Spirit to
feal us as his own, there muft be the previous
work of his grace in our hearts, as the abiding mark
of his property in us. There muft be the linea-
ments of the divine likenefs drawn in our nature,
like the lines of a fun-dial, for his light to fhine
upon, and thereby difcover to us our refemblance
of, and witnefs our relation to God, our heavenly
Father. When the holy Spirit, who has renewed
and fanctified us, irradiates his own work in our
hearts, and affures us that it is *real*, notwithftanding
its prefent imperfections, we can then triumph in
the affurance, that it will be completed in glory,
and rejoice the more fervently, the nearer we fee
ourfelves approach to that bleffed ftate. Thus I
have fhown you, what *ground* feeing God's falvation affords for a peaceful difmiffion, and have
gone through what was propofed in opening the
text.

It now remains, that I endeavour to make fome
Application of this noble fubject; not fuch as it's
importance and dignity might demand, but fuch
as the little time before us will admit; which muft
therefore be comprifed in a brief reflection, or
two. As,

I. Would

I. Would you *die in peace,* my brethren, and what an important blefling is that! how much fhould it concern you to know, whether you are the *fervants* of God, and have *feen his falvation?* Death is a folemn period, as it is the Æra or commencement of eternity, and dying work, in mere nature's ftrength, is hard work indeed; and yet it is work you will all have to do, and the great God only knows *how foon.* Of what unfpeakable importance therefore is it, to be ready and prepared for it, in the ftrength of divine grace! Now except you really bear the chara&ter of God's fervants, are, like *Simeon,* juft and devout perfons, or have cordially received *Chrift* and his falvation, you cannot die *fafely,* cannot be difmiffed of God in a way of mercy and peace, but are vi&tims for the ftroke of his vengeance. And except you have fome good *affurance* of your chriftian chara&ter, faith and experience, you cannot die *comfortably,* ferenely and joyfully. Sirs, be awakened then to give diligence, to make your calling and ele&tion fure: And may the God of grace fhew you his falvation, and fhew you feverally your perfonal intereft in it, that embracing your divine Saviour, in the arms of your faith, you may be always ready to depart in peace, and follow him chearfully into an invifible and eternal world. And,

2dly. What reafon have we to *acquiefce* in the *death* of our *chriftian friends,* and *long to follow* them, of whom we have fufficient ground to believe,

noble advice.

lieve, that they were sincere *servants* of *God*, and
had *seen his salvation*, and whom he has *dismiss'd in
peace!* Have we not parted with such, who walked
closely with God for a long course of years, who
by a holy, regular, useful and exemplary conversation, proved themselves to be the servants of
God, and shewed both *their experience*, and the
power of the gospel salvation; and who at length
received a peaceful dismission, were ready to leave
this world without any reluctance, knowing in
whom they had believed, and in hopes of going
to the enjoyment of a heavenly world? It is a
great loss the church below, and the friends and
families of God's servants sustain in their removal;
but the consideration how much it is *their gain*,
as well as *God's appointment*, should reconcile us to
it, and we should admire and adore that grace,
which made them once the excellent of the earth,
in order to make them now the blessed of Heaven.
Instead of lamenting their departure, it would be
a nobler act of christian friendship, to congratu-
late in our own breasts their safe arrival in the
presence of their beloved Saviour; whose *salvation*
they saw here, and saw enough in that to kindle
their devout affections to him, but whose glorious
person they see above, and are lost in transports of
wonder, love and joy. Having seen the end of
their conversation, let it be our great concern to
follow their faith and holiness, like them to walk
humbly and closely with God, in the exercise of
the private duties and graces of religion, and in a
serious attendance upon all its public institutions,

as

as well as to do juftice, and fhew mercy to men ; that having been ufed to converfe with our bleffed Saviour by *faith*, in his word and ordinances, and advanced in our experience of his falvation, *we* may be prepared alfo to depart in peace, and go to *fee* and *enjoy* him in his heavenly glory, along with our pious friends gone before us.

I doubt not but moft of you have anticipated me, by already applying in your own minds what has juft been faid, to the *mournful occafion* that has collected this numerous audience.—The much lamented death of the late worthy Paftor of this church, the Rev. Dr. DAVID JENNINGS. The Dr. was no friend, nor am I, to making a *practice* in funeral difcourfes, of filling up much of the time, which is appointed for the fervice of our Creator, with the hiftory, or praifes of our fellow creatures. Yet when eminent perfons, who have long filled up public ftations, with great applaufe and ufefulnefs, are removed from this world, it is fit, and may be of real ufe, that diftinguifhed notice fhould be taken of them, and fome account of them thus publicly preferved. I fhall therefore lay before you a few brief memoirs, relating to your deceafed minifter, nearly in the order in which they have been put into my hands.

The Rev. Dr. DAVID JENNINGS was the fon of the Rev. Mr. *John Jennings*, formerly of *Chrift* Church College *Oxon*, and afterwards rector of *Hartley Wafphell*, *Hants*; whence he was ejected

C   by

by the act of uniformity, on the 24th of *August* 1662, when many other excellent men also suffered for conscience sake.* He had two sons, both devoted to the ministry, and I may add, *both* ornaments to it. The elder, the Rev. Mr. *John Jennings*, was for sometime pastor of a church at *Kibworth*, in *Leicestershire*, which his father had gathered, and was afterwards tutor of an academy at *Hinckley.* Dr. *David Jennings*, the younger son, who gloried in being the *immediate* descendant of a confessor for liberty of conscience, was born *May* 18, 1691, and received his grammer learning at a free-school in *Kibworth.* About the year 1709 he came to *London*, and entered on a course of academical studies, under the tuition of the Rev. Dr. *Chauncy*, and finished them under the Rev. Dr. *Ridgley* and *Mr. Eames.* He preached his first sermon at *Battersea*, *May* 23, 1714. In *March* following he was chosen one of the lecturers, at an evening lecture then carried on at *Ro-*

aged 23

---

* He continued for some time about that county, preaching the gospel, (though at the peril of his life) whenever opportunity offered, residing probably at *Tuckwell*, where he was tutor to one Mr. *Noyes.* After that he removed into *Leicestershire*, and resided at *Langton*, as chaplain to Mrs. *Pheasant*; in whose house he founded a church of protestant dissenters, that still subsists at *Kibworth*, very near *Langton.* Dr. *Calamy* says of him, " That he was a serious and painful preacher, and of " a chearful temper; spent much time in his study, and was " well respected both by his people, and by the neighbouring " ministers, and was very easy under that retired course of " life, which he led in the latter part of his time."
Calamy's Contin. of *Baxter*, Vol. I. p. 514,15.

ther-

therhithe. In *June* 1716 he was chosen assistant to the Rev. Mr. *Foxon. May* 19, 1718, he was chosen, and *July* 25, he was ordained pastor of this church, in the room of the Rev. Mr. *Simmons* deceased. In 1719 he married Mrs. *Elizabeth Cox*;* of whom he had a melancholy loss within the year. *May* 19, 1724 he married Mrs. *Sarah Collins*†, his present mourning relict; in her he enjoyed a prudent, as well as faithful partner through life ; of whose great care and tenderness for him, under his late frequent disorder, he discovered a deep sense, and by whom he has left two sons, Mr. *Joseph* and Mr. *David Jennings.* On the decease of the Rev. Mr. *Daniel Neal,* in 1743, he was chosen a trustee of Mr. *Coward*'s large charities ; and in *August* of that year, he succeeded the Rev. Mr. *Hubbard,* as one of Mr. *Coward*'s lecturers at little St. *Helens.* On the death of the learned Mr. *John Eames* in 1744, he succeeded him as divinity professor of the academy in *London,* then chiefly supported by Mr. *Coward*'s charity ; and in *May* 1749, the ancient university of St. *Andrews* in *Scotland,* honoured him with the degree of doctor in divinity.

There are but few things of the Doctor's in print; those with his name to them, single sermons excepted, are,

* She was daugher to Mr. *William Cox* of *Wapping,* timber merchant, and died in child-bed.
† A daughter of Mr. *Joseph Collins* of *Hackney,* deceased some time before.

Ser-

Sermons to Young People, publifhed in 1730, and dedicated to his church.

Several Sermons, among thofe preach'd at *Berry Street* by feveral minifters, on the principal heads of the chriftian religion in 1733, and publifh'd in 1735.

A tranflation of profeffor *Franck*'s Letter on the moft ufeful way of preaching, and a preface, containing fome account of the profeffor; publifh'd in 1736, together with two difcourfes of Mr. *John Jennings*'s, on preaching *Chrift*, and on experimental preaching.

An Introduction to the Ufe of the Globes and Orrery, with an Appendix, attempting to explain the *Mofaic* Account of the firft and fourth days work of *Creation*; printed in 1739, but not publifh'd 'till 1747.

An Abridgment of the Life of the Rev. Dr. *Cotton Mather*, publifh'd in 1744.

An Appeal to reafon and Common Senfe, for the Truth of the Holy Scriptures, in 1755.

Befides thefe, he was author of an *anonymous* piece, written with great fmartnefs, in vindication of the fcripture doctrine of original fin, printed in 1740.

Dr. *Jennings* enjoy'd a very good ftate of health, for a great number of years, 'till within two years

of

of his death, when he was feiz'd with fits, which frequently return'd, and confiderably weaken'd him, 'till they carried him off. Upon finding himfelf decline, he was very follicitous to fee the church fettled with a paftor, capable of fupplying the lofs they fuftain'd by his incapacity of ferving them, tho' his affection for them, and not any lucrative views, made him defirous of retaining his relation to them till his death, as co-paftor with the perfon they might chufe.

After thefe brief memoirs relating to the Doctor, you may expect I fhould attempt to draw his *character*; but here I am confcious how much it muft fuffer under my hand, who am quite unpractis'd in every thing of this kind; and therefore fome fhort, imperfect fketches is all I can offer, which I hope your candour will receive, as *expreffing* my *intention*, rather than *fatisfying* my *wifh*.

Dr. *Jennings* was blefs'd with a ftrong conftitution and comely perfon, and I may fafely add, with a quick apprehenfion, an acute judgment, a lively imagination, and a happy memory. His natural temper was eafy and chearful, and at the fame time warm and fanguine; and tho' that temper always has its inconveniences, it has alfo its great advantages, which were very confpicuous in him, as it render'd him indefatigable in purfuing every ftudy he engag'd in, and indeed in filling

C 3

ing

ing up all the duties of his ftation, as they were highly his delight. His general behaviour was humane and obliging, and his converfation was very acceptable, as it was always chearful, entertaining and inftructive. For this he was well furnifh'd by his *general* knowlege; for, befides an extenfive and accurate underftanding of the Scriptures, there were few branches of fcience, or of arts and manufactures with which he was wholly unacquainted. He liv'd much in his ftudy, yet without acquiring any of the ruft and aufterity, or aukward unfocial manners which too often difgrace learning; and the ftrength of his conftitution carried him thro' a conftant feries of laborious ftudies, for feveral years after his engaging in the academy, without impairing his fpirits, or fubjecting him to that languor which attends relax'd nerves, and is apt to render perfons very uncomfortable to themfelves and others. In *private life.*——Few had the happinefs to be more valued by their friends and acquaintance; and the genuine, unaffected grief of his furviving family, fhews what a fenfe they have of their great lofs in his removal: a long courfe of harmonious years deeply endear'd him to his now afflicted confort; and he was not wanting to his children in any of the duties of an affectionate parent, which he had the pleafure to fee return'd in filial piety. He kept up the worfhip of God, and good order in his family, with great care and conftancy, and was an amiable example to them of piety, ftrict fobriety and temperance.

In

In his *public* character;—as a Minister, I need
not tell *you* of this congregation, how well fur-
nish'd he was for his work, and how acceptable in
it. As to his scheme of sentiments in divinity,
tho' he call'd no man master, but was a zealous
assertor of the right of private judgment, in op-
position to the authority of human creeds and human establishments of religion, his sentiments ⎯⎯
came nearest to *Calvinism*, as what he thought, in
the main, to be the obvious doctrine of Scripture,
and the preaching of which God had always most
remarkably own'd and succeeded. In him they
were the result of close study, which had so well
stock'd his mind with religious knowlege, that he
would often, upon occasion, preach with the same
fluency and propriety extempore, as if he had had
the greatest leisure for composing. There was
an agreeable mixture of ease and dignity in his
appearance in the pulpit; his voice was clear and
musical rather than strong; his manner graceful,
pleasing and pathetic; and his matter was so
happily diversify'd, as to render his discourses both
entertaining and edifying, ingenious and affectionate. But his *distinguishing excellency* was a cer-
tain *ease* and *perspicuity*, which ran thro' all his
performances, whether of the pulpit or the press,
by which he made every subject he treated of appear plain and familiar. He was form'd as a
preacher for a son of consolation, rather than a son
of thunder, tho' he could sometimes be awfully,
as well as tenderly pathetic. I need not tell you,
that he had a very happy gift in prayer, and could
readily adapt himself with great pertinency and

fulness

fulnefs, to the variety of cafes that occur, in common or in the chriftian life. In fhort, he was diftinguifh'd among his brethren in the miniftry for his abilities; and for many years God render'd his labours among you very fuccefsful, while with much ferioufnefs, fidelity and conftancy, he difcharg'd all the duties of his paftoral office, 'till near the clofe of his life.

It was the opinion of his diftinguifh'd abilities, procur'd him a call to the academy, from the worthy gentlemen concern'd in fupporting it, and the earneft follicitations of the ftudents, which had confiderable weight with him, to induce him to accept it. And in what a courfe of labour did that engage him! Thofe of you who had the advantage of being under his tuition, before his fatal diforder feiz'd him, well know, with what uninterrupted conftancy he fill'd up his place in the academy, never fuffering any thing to divert him from his daily attendance. You know what an eafy, happy method recommended his inftruѐtions; how familiarly he led you by the hand thro' the gates of facred truth; how affiduous he was in difcharging all the duties of his important relation to you, improving your minds with divine knowlege, recommending ferious, experimental religion to you, and watching over your manners and conduѐt; how tender he was of your interefts, and always ready to befriend and affift you! Indeed his whole foul was engag'd in his academical employ; it was his heart's defire and earneft prayer, to have his

ftudents

ftudents prove fkilful, ferious, godly minifters of
the glorious gofpel of *Chrift*; and he had the pleafure to fee many go from under his care who have
prov'd fuch, have met with great acceptance in
the world, and by whom his ufefulnefs will be as
it were prolong'd.

Thus did he chearfully perfevere in a conftant
courfe of various fervices, till it pleas'd God, about
two years fince, to permit an epileptic diforder to
feize him, probably owing to his denying himfelf fufficient reft, and over-ftraining his conftitution by *very early* ftudies, for feveral years together, after his undertaking his employ in the academy. The frequent returns of this diforder gra-
dually impair'd him, and prevented his continued
conftancy in the duties of his ftation, and made
him apprehenfive of becoming quite incapacitated
for fervice, a thing which of all others he moft
dreaded, and which he always look'd upon with
concern, when he faw it befall any of his brethren.
It was his frequent defire, that he might not out-
live his ufefulnefs; and you know how much God
was pleafed to gratify him in this; as he preach'd
the very Lord's-day before his death, and that feveral of you thought, with more fpirit than ufual.

On *Wednefday* morning, the 15th inftant, he was
vifited with a return of his fits, which, after the
convulfions went off, left him in a dozing condi-
tion, which he never came out of; but towards
evening his breath grew very fhort, and that difficulty

ficulty of breathing encreafed, 'till early on the *Thurfday* morning *, " without either figh, or groan, or the leaft ftruggling, he, in the moft eafy and compos'd manner, breath'd his laft."

Thus he departed in *peace*; and that, not only with refpect to the moft important confideration, of being in a *ftate* of *peace with God*, as he was one of his fervants, who had feen his falvation ; but alfo as to the *manner* of his dying, which was juft according to his wifh. For as his frequent fits made him apprehend his diffolution approaching, he never intimated any fear of it, but appeared habitually ready to meet it without reluctance, and often expreffed his preference of a † fudden death, if it pleafed God. And it feems, that in mercy and favour God indulged his wifh, and in the way he defired took him to himfelf. Thus he refts from his labours, and his works follow him.

And now what remains, but that we all endeavour to make a fuitable improvement of this affecting difpenfation of Providence! May you, my much refpected friends, his near relations, learn from this melancholy breach God has made upon you, to ceafe from man, to expect lefs from

---

* Dr. *Lardner*'s words, in his Funeral Sermon for Dr. *Hunt*, p. 48.

† See his Thoughts on this Subject, in his Funeral Sermon for Mrs. *Watts*, p. 16.

fellow-

fellow-creatures, and to depend more on the God
of providence and grace, to make up to you the
lofs of fo honoured and valuable a relation : be
refigned to his will, whofe *goodnefs* has appeared
in many circumftances attending this affliction,
which I need not fuggeft to you. Be thankful
your relation fubfifted fo long, with fo much comfort. And above all let it be your conftant concern, to improve the advantages you enjoyed from
his inftruction, tender care and example, that you
may follow his faith and holinefs, be the fteady,
faithful fervants of God in your day and generation, may fee his falvation, advance in the experience of its power, and fo be prepared for
being alfo difmift in peace.

As for you, my chriftian friends, the dear people of *his* charge whofe removal you now lament;
let me call upon you to be thankful, that you enjoyed a paftor above 44 years, who was capable of
almoft uninterrupted fervice among you till the
two laft, and then was not wholly laid afide; a
paftor who was fo eminently furnifhed, was fo
fkilful, faithful and diligent to ferve your fouls.
Reflect frequently on the great advantages you
enjoyed under his miniftry, ferioufly enquire what
good effect it has had upon you, and ftudy yet to
improve it. Let not his judicious and affectionate
labours among you, let not *him*, rife up againft
you at the great judgment day, to furnifh matter for your aggravated condemnation ; but be
follicitous, that through divine grace, whofe riches
you

you often heard him difplay, you may then appear with him as his joy and crown. Be ambitious
to approve yourfelves ferious, judicious, eftablifhed chriftians, worthy the privileges, worthy
the paftor, with which you have been fo long favoured; and let your behaviour as a *church* do
honour to his memory. As fuch, keep together,
walk together in love, and ftrive together in
prayer, for divine direction in your prefent circumftances; and be thankful you are not left
quite deftitute, but that you ftill enjoy the ferious,
excellent labours of your affiftant * preacher,
which I muft be free to fay, none can *flight*, without betraying a want of fenfe -or ferioufnefs; and
may the God of all grace, in his due time, fully
heal the breach he has made upon you.

And laftly, as to you my dear young friends,
far from the *laft* in *my thoughts and affections*, who
have been deprived of an excellent director of
your divinity ftudies ; let this interruption to your
ftudies, this ftate of uncertainty and fufpenfe it
has brought you into be improved, to teach you
in early life to prepare for, and calmly bear dif-
appointments, which you will frequently meet with
as you advance in life, and in a becoming deport-
ment under which, much of the ufe and credit of
religion confifts.

May you learn to look more to the great fource
of light, the author of every good gift, that di-

* The Rev. Mr. *William Ford*, junior.

vine

vine teacher, who alone teaches to profit. Commit yourfelves in ferious prayer to the divine difpofal, and on this occafion recommend it to the great head of the church, to provide proper inftruments for your further inftruction, that your education may be as happily finifh'd, as it has been ufefully begun. Be careful to make the beft ufe of the advantages you have already enjoy'd, and imitate the exemplary diligence of your late worthy tutor, in improving time, efpecially to prepare for eternity. Let it be your principal care, to cultivate an experimental acquaintance with religion, fo to fee God's falvation, and feel its power; that whenever he may call you hence, and young as you are, you know not how foon, how fuddenly that folemn event may take place, you may be ready to depart in peace.

And now, brethren, I commend you all to God, and to the word of his grace; which is able to keep you from falling, and to preferve you blamelefs, and to build you up, and to give you an inheritance among all them which are fanctify'd.

Sam: Morton Savage.   *Amen.*

The END *of the* SERMON.

THE

ORATION.

WE are now affembled upon a very *mourn-ful* occafion, to depofite in the grave the mortal part, and by this attendance to pay our laft tribute of refpect to the remains of our much efteemed, venerable friend, and father, who by the providence of God was continued to a good old age, and retained his ufefulnefs to the laft. Our grief indeed is greatly alleviated by a firm perfuafion, that his *foul* is entered into that reft which remaineth for the people of God, after the labours and fatigue of the day ; and that death fhall not have a *perpetual* dominion over his *body*, but that *it* fhall fhortly triumph over the grave by a happy and joyful refurrection to an immortal life.

It is affecting and humbling to behold the very great change, which is quickly difcovered in thefe vile bodies, when the infatiable devourer of the human race has feized us as his prey. Thofe who were once fprightly, vigorous, and active ; who have difcharged the different duties of their feveral ftations and relations in life, with great fidelity
and

and honour; and who have attracted the general notice and efteem, are inftantly deprived of all capacity for any further fervice. There is a neceffity almoft immediately to convey away the lifelefs corpfe; that in the fecret chambers of the grave, far removed from our view, it may turn to rottennefs and duft: we at length fubmit, and even become defirous, to bury our dead out of our fight. Thefe particulars can hardly fail to diftrefs us, in proportion to our apprehenfion of the excellence of the characters of our deceafed friends, and to the clofenefs of the connection, which by the awful ftroke is now diffolved.

If it was poffible to gratify our defires, we fhould joyfully extend the date of their lives far beyond the period which is affigned to the human race. We are prone ardently to wifh, that a difpenfation could be obtained in *their* favour from the king of terrors, to relieve *them* from fubmitting to the common law of mortality, which it is painful to us to think of, as befalling them; though it is an event greatly to be defired upon many accounts by themfelves, as the friends of the bleffed *Jefus*. *It is appointed to all men once to die. By one man fin entered into the world, and death by fin, and death paffes upon all men, for that all have finned.* Mournful experience convinces us abundantly, that there can be no difcharge from this warfare. The fervants of the living God, who have difcovered to

us

us the way of falvation; and thofe who have been
the moft happily diftinguifhed by eminent natural
and acquired abilities for extenfive fervice to the
intereft of religion; who have difcovered the moft
affectionate concern for the welfare of immortal
fouls; who have been the moft diligent and indefatigable in the fervice of their Mafter; who have
been crowned with the greateft fuccefs in their en-
deavours to recover men from Satan unto God;
who by their holy and upright conduct have en-
forced the doctrines and duties they have recommended to others; who have in a long, fteady,
uniform courfe of life approved themfelves the
faithful ftewards of the manifold grace of God;
even *they* are not fuffered to continue by reafon
of death. The treafure is lodged in *earthen vef-
fels*, that the excellency of the power may appear
to be of God and not of men, and that he who
glorieth may glory in the Lord; from whom pro-
ceedeth every good and perfect gift; and who efpecially commands the increafe, which attends the
labours of the minifters of his word.

But while we lament, that the prophets are not
permitted to live *for ever*; and feel the painful
ftroke which divides them from our fociety, and
deprives us of the benefit of their further inftructions; furely we fhould not fuffer them to be ab-
folutely loft to us in the *prefent* world. Being
dead they yet fpeak, by the remembrance of their
undiffembled piety and goodnefs, their holy converfation

verfation and behaviour, their attachment to the intereft of the Redeemer, and their fervent zeal or the falvation of perifhing fouls.

The Providence we are now directed to attend to, loudly calls upon *you*, my friends, who for many years have been favoured with the minif-trations of *this* faithful fervant of the bleffed Jefus, to enquire whether your improvement has been proportional to the excellency of the means of grace which *you* have enjoyed : and to be exceeding thankful, that this *burning* and *fhining* light was continued to you for fo long a feafon; and that the benefit which many of you have received from *his* labours has been exceeding great. Reflect, I intreat you, how dreadful it would be to hear *him* teftify againft any of you at the bar of God, that he ftretched out his hands all his life long to you, but you would not hear. But I hope better things of you, my brethren, though I thus fpeak, even things that pertain unto falvation : and yet from, a principle of fincere affection, I would exhort you to remember him who has had the rule over you, who has fpoken to you the word of God; whofe faith follow, confidering the end of his conver-fation ; that you all may be his crown of rejoicing in the prefence of our Lord *Jefus Chrift* at his coming.

You, my dear *young friends*, who are defigning for the important fervice of the fanctuary, will,

I per-

I perfuade myfelf, make it your *arduous endeavour*, to prove yourfelves not unworthy of thofe excellent inftructions you have received from *him*, whofe voice you will now hear no more.

This difpenfation of Providence I have no doubt will be confidered by you, the *dear relatives* of our deceafed friend, as *peculiarly* inftructive; as defigned to quicken you to be followers of him, who through faith and patience is now inheriting the promifes.

You, my *brethren* and *fathers in the miniftry*, have, I am aware, anticipated me in confidering the improvement which it becomes *us* to make of the prefent affecting ftroke : though I hope you will *bear* with me in reminding you of that which I would charge upon myfelf to lay to heart: namely, that this vifitation feems particularly calculated to animate us to employ all our talents, with our utmoft diligence for the glory of God; that we may by our increafing zeal and activity, endeavour to contribute towards repairing, in fome meafure, that lofs which the intereft of Chrift has now fuftained.

It is much to be defired, that the mournful occafion of our prefent meeting may be improved by all of us, as the means of urging us to *be always ready*. The prefent folemnity *ftrongly* enforces the advice which our Lord directs his people ever to bear in mind, to *watch*, becaufe we *know not at what hour the Son of Man will come*. The tranfition sition as to our dear friend was instantaneous, from apparent perfect health to an intire incapacity of taking any step towards his further preparation for death and judgment.

Let *each* of us then *do whatever our hands find to do with our might, because there is no device, or knowledge, or wisdom in the grave to which we haste.*

Let us *Christians* give *diligence to make our calling and election sure,* that at *whatever season* of life our Lord may summon us, or whether the degree of *warning* be greater or less, we may *depart* in *peace* ; knowing that *our Redeemer lives* ; and that though in the flesh we may see corruption, yet that *sleeping in Jesus God will bring us with him*; and that at the resurrection *this corruptible shall put on incorruption, this mortal shall put on immortality,* and that our bodies shall then be fashioned like to the *glorious Body* of our *exalted Saviour.*

Then shall the *children* of God have a most joyful meeting with *all* their *friends,* who have departed in the faith of Christ : and the *faithful minister* will receive no *inconsiderable* addition to *his* happiness and triumph in *that* day, when he shall present before the throne of God all those who had been the seals of his ministry here on earth, saying: Here am *I, and the children whom thou hast given me.*

F I N I S.

www.ingramcontent.com/pod-product-compliance
Lightning Source LLC
Chambersburg PA
CBHW031807090426
42739CB00008B/1199